AMICUS LEARNING

CHOCOLATE DELIGHTS

A Cookbook for Kids Who Love CHOCOLATE

by M. M. Eboch

AMICUS HIGH INTEREST is published by
Amicus Learning, an imprint of Amicus
P.O. Box 227, Mankato, MN 56002
www.amicuspublishing.us

COPYRIGHT © 2026 AMICUS

International copyright reserved in all countries. No part of this book may be reproduced in any form without written permission from the publisher.

LIBRARY OF CONGRESS CATALOGING-IN-PUBLICATION DATA

Names: Eboch, M. M. author
Title: Chocolate delights : a cookbook for kids who love chocolate / by M. M. Eboch.
Description: Mankato, Minnesota : Amicus Learning, [2026] | Series: Kids in the kitchen | Audience: Ages 7-10 | Audience: Grades 4-6 | Summary: "Simple dessert recipes for tweens and teens inspire kids to experiment in the kitchen. This delightful cookbook features easy-to-follow recipes for chocolate treats, including fudge, truffles, cookies, and brownies. Includes step-by-step instructions, safety tips, a glossary, and party-hosting tips"—Provided by publisher.
Identifiers: LCCN 2025019513 (print) | LCCN 2025019514 (ebook) | ISBN 9798892008693 library binding | ISBN 9798892009355 paperback | ISBN 9798896850014 ebook
Subjects: LCSH: Cooking (Chocolate)–Juvenile literature | Chocolate–Juvenile literature | LCGFT: Cookbooks
Classification: LCC TX767.C5 E326 2026 (print) | LCC TX767.C5 (ebook) | DDC 641.3/374–dc23/eng/20250429
LC record available at https://lccn.loc.gov/2025019513
LC ebook record available at https://lccn.loc.gov/2025019514

PHOTO CREDITS: Adobe Stock/Brent Hofacker, 9; Amicus/Kim Pfeffer, 7; Getty Images/The Washington Post, 10; Shutterstock/Africa Studio, 29, And-One, 4, AnjelikaGr, 24, Brent Hofacker, 19, Chatham172, 27, EasterBunny, 21, Elena Veselova, 18 (right), 25, Firanita, 14, Hanna Lepisto, 24, iuliia_n, 26, margouillat photo, 13, Monkey Business Images, 22, New Africa, 5, 11, Nina Firsova, cover, 1, Oldrich, 18 (left), Photoongraphy, 15, rontav, 30, Sergiy Kuzmin, 10, SizeSquares, 8, Tanya Sid, 12, The People's Paige, 17

EDITOR: Rebecca Glaser
SERIES DESIGNER: Kim Pfeffer
BOOK DESIGNER: Emily Dietz

CONTENTS

4
FOR THE LOVE OF CHOCOLATE

6
BEFORE YOU START

8
RECIPES

Easy Fudge 8
Chocolate Bark 10
Chocolate Sauce 12
Chocolate Raspberry Truffles 14
Chocolate Pudding Parfaits 16
Chocolate Crinkle Cookies 20
Peanut Butter Swirl Brownies 22
No-Bake Chocolate Oatmeal Cookies 26
Hot Fudge Dump Cake 28
Chocolate Satin Pie 30

32
HOST THE ULTIMATE CHOCOLATE PARTY!

FOR THE LOVE OF CHOCOLATE

If you love **CHOCOLATE**, you're not alone. People have loved chocolate for more than 5,000 years. They didn't use it in sweet desserts though. In Mexico and Central America, cocoa beans were once used as money. People there also made a drink from cocoa pods. They added honey and chili peppers for a spicy drink.

The Spanish brought chocolate to Europe in the 1500s. Some people thought it was a magical drink, good for health. Magic or not, most people like chocolate simply because it tastes so good. It comes from the seeds of cocoa pods. They are fermented, dried, and roasted to develop the wonderful taste. At this point, the seeds are bitter, so today we usually mix cocoa with sugar and milk.

Chocolate is perfect for sweet treats—from creamy pudding to rich sauces and baked goodies like cookies, brownies, and cake. These desserts are so tasty, it's tempting not to share—but your friends and family will love them just as much as you do! And when you cook them yourself, you'll impress everyone.

BEFORE YOU START

COOKING GLOSSARY

BEAT　To stir rapidly with a whisk or electric mixer to add air.

BLEND　To gently combine dry ingredients to make a smooth mixture.

BOIL　To heat a liquid until bubbles form and break at the surface or to cook in boiling water.

GREASE　To cover the surface of a baking pan with butter, oil, or cooking spray so food doesn't stick to it.

MIX　To stir until the ingredients are combined well, often combining liquids and dry ingredients.

PREHEAT　To turn on the oven before cooking, so it's at the right temperature when you put food in.

STIR　To use a spoon to loosely combine ingredients.

METRIC CONVERSION CHART

1 teaspoon (tsp.) = 5 ml

1 tablespoon (Tbsp.) = 15 ml

¼ cup = 60 ml

⅓ cup = 80 ml

½ cup = 120 ml

1 cup = 240 ml

1 quart = 1 liter

1 gallon = 4 liters

1 ounce (oz.) = 28 g

16 oz. = 460 g

GETTING READY

 Wash your hands.

 Wear an apron to protect your clothes.

 Tie back loose hair.

 Read the whole recipe first.

 Gather all your ingredients before you start.

 Ask for an adult's help if you're not sure how to do something.

HELPFUL TIPS

- **MICROWAVES** can differ in power. If you need to adjust cooking times when melting chocolate, add 15 seconds at a time.
- **COOKING TIMES** can vary. When a recipe gives a range of time, check the dish at the beginning of that range. If it's not quite done, keep cooking for a few more minutes.
- If an ingredient is listed as **DIVIDED**, it means you use it in more than one step. Make sure you use the right amount for each step.

RECIPE 1

EASY FUDGE

Soft, creamy fudge is a mouth-watering sweet treat! With just three ingredients, this quick version is super easy and delicious!

SERVINGS: 36

TIME:
- 30 minutes (prep)
- 3-4 hours (setting)

INGREDIENTS
- 12 ounces chocolate chips
- 14-oz. can sweetened condensed milk
- 1 tsp. vanilla, mint, or almond extract

EQUIPMENT
- 9 x 9-inch (23 x 23-cm) glass baking dish
- Wooden spoon
- Measuring spoons
- Sharp knife

STEPS

1. **MELT.** Pour the chocolate chips and the sweetened condensed milk into the glass pan. Microwave for 1 minute. Stir. Microwave for 1 more minute.

2. **STIR.** Add your favorite flavor of extract. Stir until the chocolate is completely melted and smooth.

3. **COOL.** Let the fudge set for several hours at room temperature until firm. Cut into 36 pieces with a sharp knife.

SPICE IT UP!

To make Spicy Mexican Chocolate Fudge, add 1 tsp. cinnamon and ¼ tsp. cayenne pepper in step 2.

RECIPE 2
CHOCOLATE BARK

Chocolate bark is crunchy and chewy. No baking, no rules—just melt, mix, and munch!

SERVINGS: 20

TIME:
- 20–30 minutes plus cooling time

INGREDIENTS
- ¾ cup nuts or seeds (pecans, almonds, pistachios, or other)
- ¼ cup dried fruit (dried cherries, cranberries, apricots, or other)
- 12 ounces chocolate chips
- 1 tsp. vegetable oil

EQUIPMENT
- Cutting board
- Sharp knife
- Microwave-safe bowl
- Parchment paper
- Baking sheet
- Silicone or rubber spatula

MAKE IT MINTY!

To make peppermint bark, use white chocolate chips and crushed candy canes.

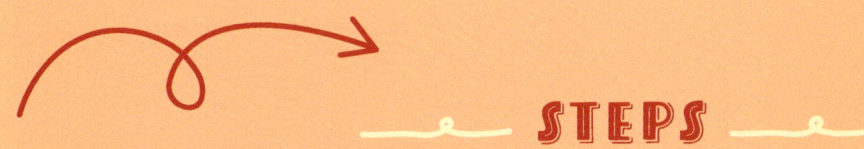

STEPS

1. **CHOP.** On the cutting board, roughly chop any large nuts or dried fruit you are using. Skip this step if you start with only small pieces of nuts and fruit.

2. **MELT AND STIR.** Put the chocolate chips and vegetable oil in a microwave-safe bowl. Microwave for 30 seconds and stir. Repeat until the chocolate is mostly melted. Then stop heating and keep stirring until the chocolate is smooth with no lumps.

3. **SPREAD.** Lay parchment paper on a baking sheet. Use the spatula to spread the chocolate in an even layer over the middle of the baking sheet. It should be about ¼ inch (0.6 cm) thick.

4. **ADD TOPPINGS.** Sprinkle the nuts and dried fruit evenly over the chocolate. Lightly press the toppings into the chocolate.

5. **COOL.** Let the chocolate bark cool until it gets hard. This takes several hours at room temperature or about 15 minutes in the refrigerator.

6. **BREAK AND SERVE.** Break the chocolate bark into about 20 pieces. You can store it in a sealed container at room temperature for up to a week.

RECIPE 3

CHOCOLATE SAUCE

This yummy sauce is ready in 5 minutes. Try it over ice cream or use it as a fruit dip.

SERVINGS: 4

TIME:
- 5 minutes

INGREDIENTS
- ¼ cup cream, milk, or water
- 1 cup chocolate chips

EQUIPMENT
- Small microwave-safe bowl
- Spoon

STEPS

1. **HEAT.** Place the cream or milk in the microwave-safe bowl. People who don't eat dairy can use water instead. Microwave for 30 seconds.

2. **MIX.** Stir in the chocolate chips.

3. **HEAT.** Microwave for another 15 seconds and stir until the chocolate is melted and smooth. Repeat if needed.

4. **SERVE.** The sauce is ready to drizzle or use as a dip!

CHOCOLATE FARMING

About 70% of chocolate comes from west Africa, where cocoa trees grow on small family farms. Buying chocolate with a Fairtrade logo helps make sure cocoa farmers get fair prices.

RECIPE 4
CHOCOLATE RASPBERRY TRUFFLES

Truffles are delicious chocolate balls, great for gifts. Roll, dip, and decorate!

SERVINGS: 24

TIME:
- about 2 hours

INGREDIENTS
- 1⅓ cups semi-sweet chocolate chips
- 2 Tbsp. heavy cream
- 2 Tbsp. butter, divided
- 2 Tbsp. seedless raspberry jam
- 1 cup milk chocolate chips
- ⅓ cup white chocolate chips

EQUIPMENT
- Heavy saucepan (a deep metal cooking pot)
- Rubber spatula
- Cookie sheet
- Aluminum foil
- Glass mixing bowls

COCOA ORIGINS

Chocolate is made from the seeds of a fruit tree. The long, yellow fruits are called pods. Cocoa pods are bright yellow and up to 1 foot (30 cm) long. Inside are small white seeds called cocoa beans. The beans turn brown after roasting.

STEPS

1. **MELT.** In a heavy saucepan, combine the semi-sweet chocolate chips, cream, and 1 Tbsp. butter. Cook over low heat, stirring the whole time with the rubber spatula until the mixture is smooth, about 5 minutes.

2. **MIX.** Stir in the raspberry jam. Freeze the mixture for 10-15 minutes.

3. **MAKE BALLS.** Spread aluminum foil over a cookie sheet. Drop spoonfuls of the mixture onto the foil-lined cookie sheet. Place the cookie sheet in the freezer for 10 minutes. Remove from freezer and roll the mixture into balls. Freeze until firm, at least 30 minutes.

4. **MELT COATING.** Put the milk chocolate chips and ½ Tbsp. butter in the mixing bowl. Microwave for 30 seconds and stir. Repeat until smooth.

5. **COAT.** Drop a truffle into the melted coating. Use a spoon to quickly stir the truffle until it is coated. Then remove the truffle, letting excess coating drip off. Place the truffle back on the cookie sheet. Repeat with each truffle.

6. **DECORATE.** Melt the white chocolate chips and ½ Tbsp. butter in a separate bowl. Microwave for 30 seconds. When smooth, drizzle over the truffles.

7. **COOL.** Chill until the truffles are firm. Store in the refrigerator.

CHOCOLATE PUDDING PARFAITS

With layers of chocolate pudding, whipped cream, and graham cracker crunch, this is a yummy—and pretty—dessert!

SERVINGS: 4

TIME:
- 25 minutes

EQUIPMENT
- Nonstick pot
- Heat-safe rubber spatula
- Parfait dishes or clear glasses
- Rolling pin
- Sealable plastic bag

INGREDIENTS
- ½ cup sugar
- 2 Tbsp. cornstarch
- ¼ tsp. salt
- 1 egg
- 2 cups milk
- 1 cup chocolate chips
- 1 1-oz. square unsweetened chocolate
- 2-3 Tbsp. butter
- 2 tsp. vanilla
- Whipped cream
- Graham crackers or cookies

STEPS

1. **BLEND.** Mix the sugar, cornstarch, and salt in the nonstick pot. Add the egg and blend very well.

2. **MIX.** Add the milk and mix well. Stir in the chocolate chips and unsweetened chocolate.

3. **HEAT.** Cook on the stove over medium heat. Stir continuously, scraping the bottom with a rubber spatula. Cook until the pudding is bubbling, thick, and smooth, 5-10 minutes.

ISLAND INSPIRATION

The idea of adding milk to chocolate comes from Jamaica. People there drank chocolate with milk 500 years ago.

4. **ADD INGREDIENTS.** Remove the pot from the heat. Add the butter and vanilla. Stir to blend well.

5. **CRUSH.** Using a rolling pin, crush the graham crackers or cookies in a sealed plastic bag.

6. **MAKE PARFAITS.** Layer pudding, whipped cream, and toppings in glasses and serve.

MORE PARFAITS!

Why stop with the basics? Layer up your favorite flavors for tasty and creative parfaits.

BANANA CREAM
LAYERS: Chocolate pudding, banana pudding, sliced bananas, and whipped cream

CHOCOLATE CAKE
LAYERS: Chocolate cake pieces, chocolate pudding, raspberries, and whipped cream

DIRT AND WORMS

LAYERS: Crumbled chocolate sandwich cookies, chocolate pudding, and gummy worms

RECIPE 6
CHOCOLATE CRINKLE COOKIES

Crackly on the outside, soft on the inside—chocolate crinkle cookies are fun to make and even better to eat!

SERVINGS: 24

TIME:
- 45 minutes

EQUIPMENT
- Large mixing bowl
- Measuring cups and spoons
- Wooden spoon or electric mixer
- Shallow bowl or pie tin
- 2 baking sheets
- Spatula

INGREDIENTS
- ½ cup (1 stick) butter, softened
- ½ cup molasses
- 1 tsp. vanilla
- ¼ cup sugar
- ½ cup cocoa powder
- 1 tsp. baking soda
- 1 tsp. cinnamon
- ¼ tsp. salt
- 1½ cups flour
- ½ cup powdered sugar to roll them in

STEPS

1. **HEAT.** Preheat oven to 350°F (180°C).

2. **BEAT.** Mix the butter, molasses, vanilla, and sugar in the mixing bowl. Add the cocoa, baking soda, cinnamon, and salt. Beat with the wooden spoon to mix well or use an electric mixer.

3. **ADD.** Stir in the flour just until blended, with no lumps showing.

4. **ROLL.** Place the powdered sugar in a shallow bowl or pie tin. Roll spoonfuls of dough into 1-inch (2.5-cm.) balls. Roll each one in powdered sugar. Place them at least 1 inch (2.5 cm) apart on the baking sheets.

5. **BAKE.** Bake 9–10 minutes until puffed and cracked. They should still look soft and gooey.

6. **COOL.** Remove from the oven and let the cookies cool for 1 minute. Then use the spatula to remove the cookies from the baking sheets.

RECIPE 7

PEANUT BUTTER SWIRL BROWNIES

Rich chocolate and creamy peanut butter come together in one super yummy, easy-to-make brownie treat!

SERVINGS: 16

TIME:
- 1 hour

INGREDIENTS
- ½ cup butter
- 1 cup white sugar
- 1 tsp. vanilla extract
- 2 large eggs
- ½ cup all-purpose flour
- ⅓ cup unsweetened cocoa powder
- ¼ tsp. baking powder
- ¼ tsp. salt
- ½ cup peanut butter

EQUIPMENT
- 9 x 9-inch (23 x 23-cm) baking dish
- 2 medium bowls (microwave safe)
- Measuring cups and spoons
- Spatula or wooden spoon
- Toothpick or butter knife

SWIRL IT!

If you don't like peanut butter, use caramel sauce or hot fudge to swirl into these brownies instead.

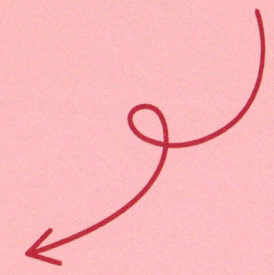

— STEPS —

1. **HEAT.** Preheat the oven to 350°F (180°C). Grease the baking dish.

2. **MIX.** Put the butter in a bowl. Heat it in the microwave just until melted, about 30 seconds. Mix in the sugar and vanilla with a spatula or wooden spoon. Blend in the eggs.

3. **BLEND.** Mix the flour, cocoa, baking powder, and salt in a separate bowl. Blend that mixture into the butter mixture.

4. **POUR.** Pour the brownie batter into the baking dish.

5. **SWIRL.** Drop small spoonfuls of peanut butter onto the brownie batter. Then use the spoon to swirl the peanut butter through the batter. Don't mix it too much. You should see the peanut butter swirls in the chocolate.

6. **BAKE.** Bake for 25 minutes. Check that a toothpick or butter knife inserted into the center comes out dry, maybe with a few crumbs attached. If the toothpick or butter knife is coated in sticky batter, bake another 5 minutes.

MORE BROWNIE FLAVOR COMBOS!

Chocolate goes with so many flavors! Which is your favorite?

WHITE CHOCOLATE SWIRL

SWIRL: Melt ½ cup white chocolate chips in microwave. Swirl into batter.

PUMPKIN SWIRL

SWIRL: Beat ½ cup pumpkin puree, 1 Tbsp. vegetable oil, and ½ tsp. pumpkin pie spice. Swirl into batter.

CHEESECAKE SWIRL

SWIRL: Beat 8 oz. cream cheese, ¼ cup sugar, 1 large egg, and ½ tsp. vanilla extract until smooth. Swirl into batter. Add berries in top layer.

RECIPE 8

NO-BAKE CHOCOLATE OATMEAL COOKIES

Whip up these rich, chocolatey cookies without baking—perfect for a hot day when you don't want to turn on the oven!

SERVINGS: 20

TIME:
- 20 minutes plus cooling time

INGREDIENTS
- 2 cups white sugar
- ½ cup butter
- ½ cup milk
- 3 cups quick cooking oats
- ½ cup cocoa powder
- 1 tsp. vanilla extract

EQUIPMENT
- Waxed paper
- 2 cookie sheets
- Medium saucepan
- Measuring cups and spoons
- Heat-safe spatula or wooden spoon

STEPS

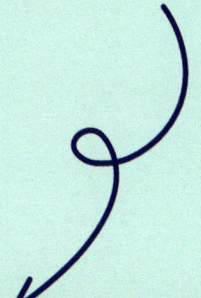

1. **PREPARE.** Lay sheets of waxed paper on cookie sheets.

2. **BLEND.** Place sugar, butter, and milk in the saucepan.

3. **HEAT.** Turn burner to medium-low. Bring mixture to a boil. Boil for 3 minutes, gently stirring with the spatula or wooden spoon the whole time. Turn off the heat and remove the saucepan from the burner.

4. **MIX.** Add the oats, cocoa powder, and vanilla. Mix.

5. **DROP.** Drop spoonfuls of the mixture onto the waxed paper on the cookie sheets.

6. **COOL.** Let cool until hardened.

RECIPE 9

HOT FUDGE DUMP CAKE

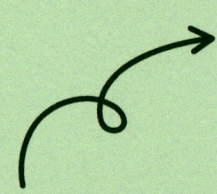

For a "dump" cake, you dump in ingredients with very little mixing. Adding hot water creates a rich pudding layer on top.

SERVINGS: 8–12

TIME:
- 1 hour

EQUIPMENT
- 9 x 13-inch (23 x 33-cm) baking dish
- Medium bowl
- Small bowl

INGREDIENTS
- 1 cup all-purpose flour
- ¾ cup white sugar
- 2 tsp. baking powder
- ¼ tsp. salt
- 6 Tbsp. baking cocoa powder, divided
- ½ cup milk
- 1 tsp. vanilla
- 2 Tbsp. vegetable oil or melted butter
- 1 cup packed brown sugar
- 1¾ cups hot water
- Serve with ice cream or whipped cream, optional

STEPS

1. **HEAT.** Preheat the oven to 350°F (180°C). Grease the baking pan.

2. **DUMP.** In the medium bowl, dump in the flour, sugar, baking powder, salt, and 2 Tbsp. of the cocoa powder.

3. **BLEND.** Stir in the milk, vanilla, and oil or melted butter. Blend until smooth. Spread the mixture evenly into the baking pan.

4. **MIX TOPPING.** In the small bowl, mix the brown sugar and the remaining 4 Tbsp. (¼ cup) cocoa powder. Sprinkle this mixture on top of batter.

5. **POUR.** Gently pour the hot water over everything. Do not mix it in.

6. **BAKE.** Bake the cake. Check it at 30 minutes to see if the center is almost set. It should look like a lumpy mixture of cake and pudding. If the cake parts aren't yet firm, continue cooking, checking every 5 minutes. Serve warm with ice cream or whipped cream.

RECIPE 10

CHOCOLATE SATIN PIE

Smooth, rich, and chocolatey—this no-bake pie is easy to make and melts in your mouth like magic!

SERVINGS: 8

TIME:
- 40 minutes (prep)
- 3 hours (refrigeration)

INGREDIENTS
- 1½ cups chocolate cookie or graham cracker crumbs
- 6 Tbsp. butter
- 1 12-oz. can evaporated milk
- 2 large egg yolks
- 2 cups semi-sweet chocolate chips
- Whipped cream, optional

EQUIPMENT
- Food processor, or large plastic bag that zips closed plus a rolling pin
- Mixing bowl
- Pie pan
- Medium saucepan
- Heat-safe spatula or wooden spoon

COCOA MATH

It takes 400 cocoa beans to make 1 pound (453 grams) of chocolate! It's a good thing each cocoa tree can make about 2,500 beans each year.

STEPS

1. **CRUSH.** Make the crust first. Crush the cookies or graham crackers in a food processor or in a sealable plastic bag with a rolling pin.

2. **MIX AND PRESS.** In a mixing bowl, microwave the butter until melted, checking and stirring every 20 seconds. Add the crumbs and mix with the melted butter. Pour into pie pan and press evenly around the bottom and sides.

3. **BLEND.** Put the evaporated milk and egg yolks in the saucepan and blend with the heat-safe spatula or wooden spoon.

4. **HEAT.** Cook on the stove over medium-low heat. Gently stir as the mixture gets hot and starts to thicken, 5 to 8 minutes. Do not let it boil. If you start to see bubbles, turn down the heat.

5. **STIR.** Remove the pot from heat. Stir in the chocolate chips until they are completely melted and the mixture is smooth and fully blended.

6. **COOL AND TOP.** Pour the mixture into the crust. Refrigerate until firm, about 3 hours. Top with dollops of whipped cream before serving, if you like.

HOST THE ULTIMATE CHOCOLATE PARTY!

Want to throw a sweet **CHOCOLATE** party your friends will remember? Learn to be a great host!

- **GUEST LIST/FOOD ALLERGIES:** Start by making a guest list. Ask about food allergies, such as nuts or diary. You might even know someone allergic to chocolate. Make sure you have treats for everyone!
- **CHOOSE YOUR MENU:** Decide which recipes to make ahead. You can make some recipes with guests. Chocolate bark is a good one to make with friends. You might make pudding ahead of time and let people build their own parfaits.
- **BE A GOOD HOST:** Greet everyone with a friendly smile. If some people don't know each other, introduce them. Help everyone feel comfortable.
- **ACTIVITIES:** Play chocolate charades. Write scenes like "making hot chocolate" or "eating a melting chocolate bar" on slips of paper. Guests act out the scenes and people guess what they are. Laughs and teamwork make parties fun.
- **CLEAN UP:** When the party's over, ask everyone to help clean up. It's easier and more fun if you do it together! You can send guests home with goodie bags holding truffles and pieces of fudge.

With these tips, your chocolate party will be sweet and fun!